THE PANAMA CANAL
IN AMERICAN HISTORY

Other titles *in American History*

IN
AMERICAN
HISTORY

THE PANAMA CANAL
IN AMERICAN HISTORY

Ann Graham Gaines

Enslow Publishers, Inc.
40 Industrial Road   PO Box 38
Box 398   Aldershot
Berkeley Heights, NJ 07922 Hants GU12 6BP
USA   UK
http://www.enslow.com

Library of Congress Cataloging-in-Publication Data

Gaines, Ann.
    The Panama Canal in American history / Ann Graham Gaines.
        p. cm. — (In American history)
    Includes bibliographical references and index.
    Summary: Examines the planning, building, and maintenance of
the Panama Canal and its current status.
    ISBN 0-7660-1216-6
    1. Panama Canal (Panama)—History—Juvenile literature.
    2. Americans—Panama—History—Juvenile literature. [1. Panama
Canal (Panama)] I. Title. II. Series.
    F1569.C2G25 1999
    972.87′5—DC21   98-14477
                                            CIP
                                            AC

Printed in the United States of America

10 9 8 7 6 5 4 3

Illustration Credits: Willis J. Abbot, *Panama and the Canal: In Pictures
and Prose* (London: Syndicate Publishing Company, 1913), pp. 67, 87;
Arthur Bullard, *Panama: The Canal, the Country, and the People* (New
York: Macmillan, 1912), pp. 13, 43, 63; *Century Magazine*, vol. XLI,
no. 119, p. 31; Corel Corporation, pp. 8, 55; Enslow Publishers, Inc.,
pp. 15, 59, 84, 103; *Harper's New Monthly Magazine*, vol. XVIII, no.
CIV, January 1859, pp. 46, 48, 50, 52; *Harper's New Monthly Magazine*,
vol. XVIII, no. CVI, March 1859, pp. 20, 21, 23; National Archives,
p. 74; The Panama Canal Commission, *The Panama Canal Review*,
Winter 1977, pp. 80, 81, 91, 98, 99, 100, 105, 109; Reproduced from
the *Dictionary of American Portraits*, published by Dover Publications,
Inc., in 1967, pp. 78, 89.

Cover Illustrations: Corel Corporation; Willis J. Abbot, *Panama and
the Canal: In Pictures and Prose* (London: Syndicate Publishing
Company, 1913); Arthur Bullard, *Panama: The Canal, the Country, and
the People* (New York: Macmillan, 1912).

★ CONTENTS ★

THE CANAL BETWEEN THE OCEANS

If you look on a map of the Western Hemisphere near the bottom of Central America, just before a tiny teardrop of land expands into the massive head of South America, you will see Panama. The country of Panama is very narrow, stretching only sixty miles wide between the Atlantic and Pacific oceans. In 1914 the United States finished building a canal across this narrow isthmus. To many people who stand on the deck of a large oceangoing ship passing through this canal, the transit is one of the most unusual and beautiful experiences of their lives.

A typical passage from the Atlantic to the Pacific Ocean begins as the ship leaves the ocean harbor at Colón and enters a narrow channel bordered by a canopy of rain forest trees and vines. The sudden change of colors, from the subdued slate blues of the sea to the lively greens of the jungle, makes the passenger aware that the ship, accustomed to the immense open spaces of the sea, is now coming into something close, strange, and amazing. Soon the ship slows down and stops. Steel lines are passed between the ship and towing locomotives. The lines are made tight. Then the ship is pulled into a 1,000-foot-long chamber, called a lock, by the locomotives moving on tracks on the lock's concrete walls, which rise nearly fifty feet above the water level of the ship. Massive iron doors noiselessly swing shut behind the ship. The ship begins to rise as millions of gallons of water are allowed to bubble up through the chamber floor, pushing the ship up as the water level rises in the lock. Soon the passenger on deck can see out over the top of the chamber and into the surrounding jungle, which comes up to within ten yards of the sides of the locks. When the ship reaches the top of the lock, the

This is a view of ships moving through the Panama Canal.

passenger can see another lock in front of the ship. As the level of water in the two adjoining locks becomes equal, the massive steel gates between them open, as if by magic, and the locomotives pull the ship into position in the second lock. Then the doors behind it close again. For a second time the passenger looks out upon massive concrete walls on each side of the ship. The whole process to fill the lock with water is repeated. Then the ship is pulled through yet a third lock. The entire trip through the three locks takes less than an hour to complete. When the gates of the third lock open, the ship sails out onto a huge freshwater lake, Gatun Lake, that sits 85 feet above sea level and covers more than 185 square miles.

The water in Gatun Lake is green, not blue or gray. Because it is freshwater, it kills all the ocean barnacles on the sides and bottoms of the ships that pass through it. From the low-lying islands near the route of the ship across the lake, colorful parrots and other tropical birds fly, cry, and nest in the tops of the jungle trees. Soon the ship reaches Gamboa. There, it enters a very narrow, nine-mile-long channel that cuts between the mountains of the Continental Divide. These mountains rise several hundred feet above the ship and seem to press down closely to ships as they pass through. The water in this Culebra Cut is brown from the constant mud slides that come down the mountainsides. There is little wind or noise in the cut. A passenger may experience an eerie sense that no ship belongs so close to mountaintops. At the end of the cut, there are more locks to bring the ship back down to sea level. The ship is positioned in a full lock and all the doors close. The water is then allowed to flow out through the same holes in the floor of the lock that were used to fill it. The ship is lowered until the walls of the lock rise high above the top of the ship, and the water level of the lock matches the level on the Pacific Ocean side. The seaside gate is then opened and the ship passes beyond. When the ship passes through the last of the three locks on the Pacific Ocean side at Miraflores, it enters a sea-level channel that leads to the ocean harbor at Panama City.[1]

The entire trip between the oceans can be made during the light of one day. Using the canal saves eight thousand miles on a journey between the oceans. When the canal was almost finished, a commission in the United States was sent to Panama to see how the completed project could be made more beautiful. The commission, whose members included some of the most noted artists and architects of the time, wrote in its report:

> The canal, like the Pyramids or some imposing object in natural scenery, is impressive from its scale and simplicity and directness. One feels that anything done merely for the purpose of beautifying it would not only fail to accomplish that purpose, but would be an impertinence.[2]

The dream of this beautiful canal had existed in the minds of people almost since the discovery of the narrow Isthmus of Panama by Europeans. The canal seems almost a natural part of the landscape. It has only a few moving parts and a few sets of gates to identify it as man-made. The actual construction of the canal took more than fifty years to complete. Over twenty-five thousand people died in the effort. Today, the passage through the jungle from ocean to ocean reveals nothing of that colossal struggle. This book tells that story.

2

THE DISCOVERY OF PANAMA AND THE PACIFIC

In December 1502, Christopher Columbus, who discovered the New World in 1492, was searching for a channel or passageway through the lands he had recently discovered when he sailed along the coast of Panama on his fourth voyage. In his three previous voyages from Spain, Columbus had discovered many new islands. But these new discoveries just stood in the way of his real goal. He wanted to reach the Spice Islands and China.

On January 6, 1503, Columbus anchored his four ships off the coast of Panama at the mouth of a river he named the Río Belén, or River Bethlehem.[1] There, naked Indian warriors—whose bodies were painted in red, yellow, blue, and black with figures of birds and animals—came down to the shore to meet Columbus and his crew. The Indians were armed with spears, bows and arrows, and shields.[2] They were friendly and were willing to trade the small golden trinkets they wore for cheap bells and glass beads. Their gold quickly diverted Columbus's attention from his search for a route to the Spice Islands and China.

The Spanish Discover Panama

Columbus sent his brother, Bartholomew Columbus, with sixty-eight men and some friendly Indian guides to search for more gold. As the Indians led them through the jungle near shore, they often found places where tiny flakes of gold could be seen lying in the streams. The Spaniards, never satisfied with finding just a little bit, wanted to go on and find the source of those flakes, the mother lode. Their Indian guides quickly tired of searching for a metal they valued very little. They soon led the Spaniards back to the coast. Thereafter, Columbus's men abused the Indians, stealing their gold and hurting their women and children. From then on, the Indians mistrusted and

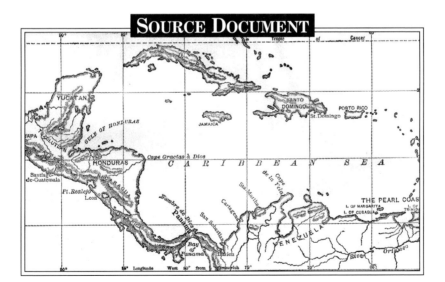

SOURCE DOCUMENT

This map of the Caribbean Sea, made during the sixteenth century, shows some of the areas explored by Christopher Columbus.

hated the European invaders of their homeland. They did not often fight openly with the invaders, for the Europeans had steel armor and weapons the natives could not defeat: guns, swords, and vicious dogs. Instead, they simply disappeared into the jungle as the Europeans approached. When they did meet, the natives would lie and deceive the Spaniards at every opportunity.

Without the Indian guides and their knowledge, the Europeans saw Panama as a hostile and dangerous land. Men would walk a hundred yards into the rain forest and disappear forever. The Spaniards learned to stay on the coast, in sight of the sea. Finally, the Indians rose up and attacked the Spaniards, forcing them to leave the area. Christopher Columbus returned to Spain. He never knew that he had been only sixty miles from what he so desperately sought— just sixty miles across Panama lay another ocean and open passage to China.[3]

Where Is Panama?

On a modern map, the Isthmus of Panama runs from east to west. This seems strange to us, not fitting in with our mental map. We visualize South America as sitting directly south of North America, hanging, as it were, by a thread. But that is not so. Instead, it is as if the giant landmasses of North and South America twist this tiny isthmus that joins them.

The reason for this peculiar geography lies in the very distant past. North and South America have not

This map shows the location of Panama, the narrow isthmus between the continents of North and South America.

always been joined together. In fact, South America was once part of Africa. Over millions of years, what is now South America broke off from the continent of Africa and drifted to the west. As this new continent came closer to North America, plate tectonics caused them to push up the bottom of the seabed between them. (According to the theory of plate tectonics, movement of semirigid sections of the earth's crust has resulted in continental drift and changes in the size and shape of continents and oceans.)

Thus was formed much of what is now Central America and the Isthmus of Panama. As they approached each other from the east and west, the newly created land between them stretched east and west. So what we see on the map today as one land-mass that exists from Alaska in the north to Tierra del Fuego in the south is really three landmasses that have gradually come together.[4]

Panama's Rain Forest

The Panama rain forest looked in the time of Columbus much as it does today. On the Atlantic Coast, giant low-lying mangrove swamps formed a swampy area between the ocean and the land. Where the rivers flowed out into the ocean, the water was salty and undrinkable. One wrong, unsure step would cause a traveler to sink into ooze up to his armpits as he climbed around and through the tangled roots of the crowded, towering trees that formed the shady canopy above. What looked like safe places to stand would turn out to be pockets of quicksand, which would entirely swallow anyone who stepped into them.

As one penetrated farther south into the jungle, the land rose and the swamp gave way to an area where the footing was more sure. Here, the jungle floor was a soft, damp mat of decaying plants and dead leaves. There were no trails. It was quiet, hot, and wet. This was a land of even denser rain forest, where hundreds of different species of trees and plants were packed so tightly together that you could not walk unless you cut a passage with a machete, a two-foot-long knife. Within days, new growth would seal your path shut again. Vines with two-inch stickers like iron spikes ripped the clothes off a traveler's back as he fell, entangled, to the ground.

Here lived coral snakes, fer-de-lance, and bushmasters, three of the most poisonous snakes in the world. Jaguars and pumas stalked the jungle floor. It was not the large animals that were the most dangerous, however; it was the small ones. Army ants moved in millions and ate anything in their path. Spiders, sand flies, chiggers, and thousands of other still-unnamed bugs crawled over every part of a passerby, inside and outside every bit of clothing, mask, or net worn in defense. Mosquitoes, so thick they would put out a candle light, carried an even more deadly and unseen killer: disease. Yellow fever and malaria, borne in the bite of the mosquito, would strike, causing high fevers and agonizing pain. For most, it would be over quickly—they died. Those who survived remained exhausted for months.[5]

The Indians knew how to walk, even run, through this natural barrier, but they usually traveled by canoe on the area's many waterways. Deeper into the jungle, the land continued to rise slowly until it reached the peaks of low mountains, approximately twenty miles from the ocean. These peaks were only two to three hundred feet high in some places.

The Continental Divide

The highest elevation between the oceans of any continent is known as the Continental Divide. The tops of the peaks rising from the Panamanian jungle form the Continental Divide. On one side, the streams created by rain flow north into the Atlantic Ocean. The rain that falls just a few feet away, on the other side, flows south into the Pacific. The line that marks the Continental Divide runs through the continents of North and South America. In North America the Continental Divide runs through the Rocky Mountains. The rain that falls on the eastern side of the mountain peaks empties into the Mississippi River, which flows thousands of miles before it empties into the Atlantic Ocean. In South America the Continental Divide runs along the peaks of the Andes Mountains. The vast Amazon River gathers the rain that falls on the eastern slopes of Peru and Bolivia and carries it thousands of miles across Brazil to the Atlantic Ocean. In Panama, these distances are compressed tightly. It is only forty-five miles from the Continental Divide to the Atlantic Ocean; it is only fifteen miles before the jungle gives way to the sandy beaches of the Pacific Ocean.

Balboa Discovers the Pacific Ocean

Vasco Núñez de Balboa had been a young crewman in the two-ship expedition to the New World of Rodrigo Bastides of Seville in 1501. The members of this expedition were the first Europeans to sail by the coast of Panama, a year before Columbus. Balboa returned to Hispaniola after this expedition. (Today the island of Hispaniola is divided between the nations of Haiti and the Dominican Republic—in the sixteenth century, it served as headquarters for the Spanish in the New World.)

Balboa was unlucky and made an enemy of the governor of the island. In 1509 Balboa fled the country, hidden in a wine cask carried aboard a ship preparing to depart on an expedition in search of slaves. Poisoned Indian arrows and disease almost completely wiped out the expedition along the northern coast of South America. The few men who survived fled under the leadership of Balboa.

Balboa took the men to Panama and landed at the site of a deserted Indian village that the Spanish renamed Santa María de la Antigua del Darién. The name both honored the mother of Jesus and used the Indian name for the river Darién that flowed nearby. Balboa was a natural leader. At this time he was said to

This is an artist's depiction of Balboa escaping from the governor of Hispaniola in a wine cask.

be "thirty-five years of age, tall, well-shap'd and limb'd, strong, of a good Aspect, fair-hair'd, ingenious, and patient under Hardship."[6]

Balboa soon organized his new colony and began raiding Indian villages along the coast of Panama, looking for gold. On one of these expeditions, he captured an important chief named Careta. Through Spanish survivors of the ill-fated Panama expedition who had learned the Cuna Indian language, Balboa had long conversations with Careta and came to respect and honor him. Balboa made an alliance with Careta and even married Careta's daughter in an Indian ceremony. Balboa's respect for all the local natives increased. He stopped raiding and formed alliances with the various chiefs who lived along the coast.

Balboa did not, however, stop looking for gold. In one of the villages of his new allies, a young chief named Comagre told the Spanish that they were fools to desire gold so much, for it was worthless; but if they still wanted it, he could help them. He told them of a land across the Isthmus. There, he said, lived "cannibal goldsmiths" who sailed on another vast ocean in ships as large as the Spaniards'. To conquer them would, he thought, take an army of one thousand soldiers and the

Balboa forged alliances with some of the Indians living along the coast of Panama. He even married an Indian princess in a ceremony depicted here.

help of many local Indian tribes. Balboa sent back to Hispaniola for more men to help him. When word came that the men were coming, not to help in the new adventure, but rather to arrest him, Balboa set out with the 190 men he already had and his Indian allies. They marched south into the jungle at the end of August 1513.

Even with Indians to carry the supplies and guide the way, the Spanish explorers could march only about a mile a day through the jungle. The Spaniards always wore their heavy helmets and armor because they feared sudden attack. They would sometimes meet hostile Indian tribes they had to fight. The Spaniards quickly demonstrated the power of their steel armor and swords, and achieved peace. Soon more than half of the men were left behind, however, exhausted from the heat, poisoned by the snakes, and sick from the diseases they caught from constant insect and spider bites. Amazingly, no one died.

Finally, on September 26, with only sixty-six men left, Balboa led his men to the top of a hill and stopped in wonder. Before him, he could see the vast blue expanse of a new ocean, water as far as he could see to the horizon, perhaps never before seen by a European. He knew it was the passage to China, the passage that Columbus himself had sought for so many years. Balboa knelt down to pray. He thanked God for giving the glory of this discovery to him, an ordinary man without experience or authority. All his men came to the top of the hill. They, too, knelt in prayer, thanking God and congratulating each other. It took them several more days to cut their way down from the Continental Divide through the jungle to the beach. At the water's edge, Balboa waded waist deep into the water wearing his battle armor and formally claimed the ocean and all the lands that touched it in the name of the king of Spain. Since they had come from the north, Balboa called the new ocean the South Sea.[7]

Balboa claimed all of the Pacific Ocean for the king of Spain.

Pizarro Discovers Gold in Peru

In 1532, Francisco Pizarro, one of the men who had knelt on top of the hill when they first saw the Pacific Ocean, conquered that tribe of cannibal goldsmiths that Comagre, the Indian chief, had spoken of.[8] They were the Incas of Peru. Unlike the Indians of Panama, they had not just a few gold trinkets, but tons of gold. The Spaniards took all they could find and shipped it back to Spain, making Spain the richest nation on earth for a hundred years. All this gold was shipped across the Isthmus of Panama, across the same sixty miles of jungle that had taken Balboa two months to cross. The treasure was carried by boat to Panama, unloaded and taken by mule train across the Isthmus, and loaded once again into other ships that carried the gold to Spain.

Over the next two hundred years, as the Spanish empire spread across the Pacific Ocean, no one knows how much wealth was carried across Panama. Vast quantities of gold were taken from Peru. Sea chests full of pearls came from the Philippines. Between 1545 and 1600, 50 million pounds of silver were sent from Bolivia to Spain. The king of Spain, of course, wanted to protect the vast treasure that was coming across Panama. The idea of a canal across the Isthmus that would allow a ship to carry its load of treasure all the way to Spain from where it was first loaded was very attractive.[9]

Transporting Gold Across Panama

As early as 1526, even before the conquest of Peru, the governor of Panama, which was then called Castilla del Oro, or the "Castle of Gold," was instructed to search for an easier route across the Isthmus. In 1527, Captain Hernando de la Serna reported that the Chagres River, the largest in the area, was navigable by canoe and flat-bottomed boats for almost twenty miles from its headwaters near the Continental Divide north to where it emptied into the Atlantic Ocean. Serna also reported that a road for carts could be hacked out of the jungle from the Chagres River, over the Continental Divide, and down the fifteen miles to the Pacific Coast.

In 1534, Charles V, then king of Spain, ordered a survey to see if a water canal could be opened that would extend the Chagres River down the Pacific side of the Continental Divide to the ocean. One of the officials of Panama, Pascual de Andagoya, was in charge of this survey. He wrote the king that he would do as the king ordered, but that nothing could be accomplished until the rainy season was over. He stated that this project could only have been advised by a man who was totally ignorant of the country. He went on to say that no prince in this world, no matter how powerful, could unite the two seas, or even pay its staggering cost. He deemed it possible, however, to maintain a road connection between the Chagres River and the Pacific Ocean at a little cost with a few workers.[10] Andagoya offered the king perfectly good advice, but the idea of a short canal that would accomplish so much did not go away.

In 1555, the idea for the canal had been published in the book, *The Discoveries of the World* by Antonio Galvaõ, the Portuguese governor of the Moluccas Islands (once known as the Spice Islands, these islands are part of Indonesia and were settled by the Portuguese).[11] When Philip II, the son of Holy Roman Emperor Charles V, became the king of Spain in 1556, he began to hear much about the idea of a Panama canal. Francisco López de Gómara, the chaplain of Hernán Cortés (the Spanish explorer who conquered the Aztecs), wrote a letter to the new king, urging him to construct a canal either in Panama or Nicaragua.[12] King Philip realized that the world knew about and was discussing what to do with *his* very valuable and private Pacific Ocean treasure route. He did not want anyone else to have access to—or be able to steal—his treasures. He immediately stopped all official talk of a Spanish canal across Panama.

His successor, Philip III, who ascended the Spanish throne in 1598, also considered digging a canal across Panama but was dissuaded when his advisors pointed out how likely a canal would be to attract enemies and how difficult it would be to defend. For the next two hundred fifty years, Spain ruled Central and South America, and while it did, Spanish officials talked no more of the Panama Canal. Still, the idea would not die.

THE GOLD RUSH OF 1849

From the beginning of the sixteenth century until the beginning of the nineteenth century, while Spain maintained control over its vast empire in the Western Hemisphere, no one was allowed to build a canal, or even a road wide enough for an ox-drawn cart to pass, across the Isthmus of Panama. This did not stop people from talking or dreaming about it, however.

A Great Mind Considers a Canal

One of the most famous scientists of the time, Alexander von Humboldt of Prussia, wrote about building a canal to join the Pacific and Atlantic oceans. From 1799 to 1804, Humboldt roamed South and Central America under a most unusual passport granted him by Charles IV, the king of Spain. He was allowed to inspect whatever he wanted. Just before he returned to Europe, Humboldt spent three weeks as a guest of President Thomas Jefferson of the United States. Jefferson must have been amazed at the vast knowledge of geography that Humboldt had amassed during his travels. In a book, *Political Essay on the*

Kingdom of New Spain, published in 1811, Humboldt discussed the most likely route for an interoceanic canal. He thought that a site across Nicaragua was the best route. In fact, Humboldt thought that a canal across Panama was, because of physical obstacles, the worst possible choice. Humboldt's book influenced many of the leading thinkers of his day.

Soon after the publication of Humboldt's book, the old, decaying Spanish empire crumbled. It had run short of money and faced rebellions in many of its colonies. By 1825, Spain no longer controlled any provinces in Central or South America. What are now Panama and Colombia then formed a country called New Granada, whose capital was Bogotá, now the capital of Colombia. A little more than twenty years later, the attention of the United States and the rest of the world returned to the narrow Isthmus of Panama and its short overland journey between the oceans.[1]

The Gold Rush

Rumors started to spread across the United States in 1848. Throughout a large area of country on the Pacific Coast, the valleys and ravines showed the presence of vast deposits of nuggets and particles of pure gold, often in plain sight. A slight excavation of the soil revealed far richer deposits beneath. The area was thinly populated, and the field was open to all who could get there. On December 5, 1848, the president of the United States, James Knox Polk, sent a message to the members of Congress in Washington,

D.C., announcing to the country that the rumors were true.[2] The governor of California, a territory that had entered the United States under the Treaty of Guadalupe Hidalgo in 1848, had sent a bag full of gold nuggets to the president as proof.[3] The news immediately spread to the newspapers and electrified the nation. Thousands of people started for California. It was generally believed that anyone who could wield a pick, a shovel, and a tin pan for washing the dirt off the gold could be sure of large returns, with the chance of a fortune.

Routes to California

There were several routes to California for the new "Argonauts," the name given to these adventurers. Reaching California overland across the country was very dangerous. The maps of that time showed all the territory west of the state of Missouri as a blank, across which were printed the words, "Great American Desert." This desert was shown on the map to go all the way to the Pacific Coast.[4] Moreover, overland travel was impossible until May or June when the warmer spring weather would melt the snow and ice that covered the land and mountains.

There remained two water routes to California: one around the Horn, as the tip of South America was called, and one across the Isthmus of Panama. The trip around the Horn to California was very long, almost thirteen thousand miles, and it, too, was very dangerous: The Straits of Magellan at the tip of South America were almost always stormy. High waves and winds often turned ships away from the passage. Shipwrecks were not uncommon. The route across Panama was much shorter, about four thousand miles from New Orleans, but it required the traveler to leave the ship that had brought him from the United States at an Atlantic port of Panama, travel overland the sixty miles to the Pacific Ocean, and then catch another ship north to California.[5] The Isthmus was then an unknown wilderness, crossed occasionally by traders and adventurers in canoes on the Chagres River a part of the distance and then by mule train to the Pacific Coast. The Pacific Mail Steamship Company had recently formed. It had sent two ships, the *Oregon* and the *California,* around the Horn to establish regular mail and passenger service between Panama City and California.[6]

Forty-niners Land in Panama

By the end of January 1849, a little over a month after the president's address, ten ships, four steamships, and six sailing vessels had landed 726 men, bound for California, at the mouth of the Chagres River. It was a dangerous landing, because there was no port. The men had to be rowed ashore through the high waves in dugout canoes manned by the natives from the beach. All these men made the perilous trip across the Isthmus and tried to buy passage north on the *California*.

But the *California* was designed to carry only 250 passengers. Furthermore, it already had a few

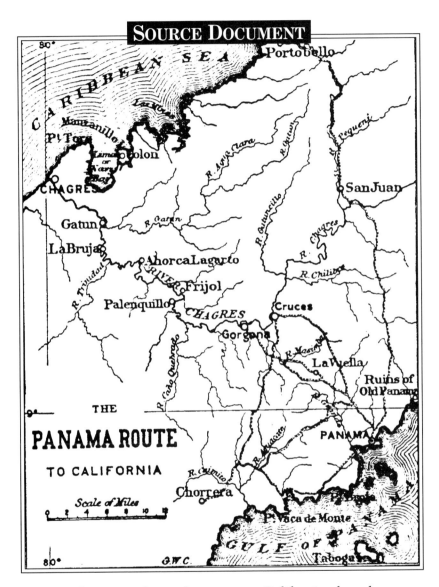

This map shows the route to California through Panama used during the gold rush of 1849.

passengers who had boarded in New York or New Orleans as well as about fifty Peruvians who had boarded when the ship stopped in Callao, Peru, on its way around South America. Many of the waiting Americans wanted to throw the Peruvians off the ship since they were not citizens of the United States, and take their places. The Peruvians, of course, would not leave. The crisis was finally resolved by hastily building extra cabins on the deck and taking as many of the waiting Americans as was possible without sinking. The ship left with about 365 very crowded passengers.[7] Of course, this left just as many would-be miners waiting on the beach for the next ship to arrive. And wait they did, because ships on the west coast of South America were few and far between. When the *California* docked in San Francisco Bay on February 28, everyone—the passengers and the entire crew except for the captain—left the ship immediately for the goldfields.

When the other ship of the Pacific Mail Steamship Company, the *Oregon,* reached Panama City on February 23, there were 1,200 men waiting to book passage north. The *Oregon* sailed north on March 13 with only 250 of those men. The others had to wait. There were plenty of ships to bring the '49ers, as those who went to California during the gold rush were nicknamed, to Panama. There simply were not enough ships in all of the Pacific Ocean to transport the men waiting there to California.[8] It was such a short distance of sixty miles across the Isthmus of Panama. If only there were a canal across those sixty miles, a single ship could sail from New York to San Francisco without going all the way around South America. It would be much quicker and safer.

The Trip Across Panama

The route across the Isthmus was not like anything these "Yankees" from the United States had ever seen before. The first part of the trip was made in canoes up the Chagres River. These canoes, called bungos, had been dug out of a single tree trunk, twenty or more feet long and three to four feet wide. The bungos, with several passengers sitting underneath a canvas awning for protection against the tropical sun, were pushed upstream by Indians using long poles. It was hard work.

In the dry season, from December to May, the bungos could ascend the Chagres River as far as Gorgona, a native village almost forty miles from the Atlantic Ocean. During the rainy season, from June to November, the bungos could go as far as Cruces, another native village about four miles up the river.

The trip upriver usually took three to four days, depending on the skill of the native crew. At night the travelers would stop at native huts along the way where they could buy supper and a hammock to sleep in. The cost of the trip was about five to ten dollars in the currency of the day for each passenger.[9] The trip up the Chagres was a marvelous adventure for the North Americans. The rich green jungle came right down to the clear water of the river. The boatmen sang native songs to keep their poles in cadence as they labored upstream against the current. The monkeys, savage beasts, and birds that could often be seen in the jungle nearby answered the boatmen with strange cries and howls. Large alligators swam beside the boat, looking for lunch.[10]

The trip up the Chagres River ended at either of the small towns of Gorgona or Cruces. Then travelers for California would pack their goods and provisions on a mule or on the back of a native Indian, and walk the twenty miles down the Pacific side of the Continental Divide. Each mule or native porter cost about twenty dollars for the trip. Few miners had brought enough spare money to ride either on a mule or slung in a hammock between two Indians, so while they paid to have their luggage carried down to the ocean, they themselves walked.[11] Many of the miners wrote letters home that told of the beauties of the swarms of blue butterflies, the brilliant green mountains, and the picnic lunches they enjoyed.

The trip across the Isthmus could be a beautiful, exciting adventure. For others, however, it proved a difficult journey. One traveler wrote home:

> I have no time to give reasons, but in saying it I utter the united sentiments of every passenger whom I have heard speak, it is this, and I say it in fear of God and the love of man, to one and all, for no consideration come this route. I have nothing to say for the other routes but do not take this one.[12]

Although he offers no details, his letter probably reflects the fact that the trip could be a horrible, desperate struggle for life. Mostly, it depended on the rain.

The Rainy Season

From December to May, clear skies and breezy tradewinds made every day a warm delight. In April and May, large cumulus clouds would gather in the skies during the afternoon. By the middle of June, a little rainstorm would come every few days. By the summer, the rain clouds would gather a little bit earlier in the day, the rain would come a little earlier, and it would rain a little harder and a little longer. By the beginning of fall, there would be a torrential storm every day, dropping two to three inches of rain within one hour. Some days it would rain all afternoon. By November a foot or two of rain could fall in a single day. Then, suddenly, it would be over. Just when it would appear as if all the land would be washed out to sea, the rains would stop. It would not rain again for four or five months.[13]

During the rainy season, streams would form all over the land and flow into the local rivers. The Chagres River was the largest of the local waterways. Its headwaters were near the Continental Divide and flowed swiftly down through limestone channels into the lower lands of the Isthmus. The rivers and the streams that flowed into the Chagres covered most of the Isthmus, nearly thirteen hundred square miles (roughly the size of the state of Rhode Island). During a normal rain, the river would often rise ten feet in a single day. The river's water would overflow its banks for half a mile in each direction, tearing tree trunks out of the ground and washing them downstream. Animals and insects would flee in desperation. The treetops would turn black as millions of tarantula spiders climbed to the very top of the forest canopy.

In one heavy rain that lasted three days, the river rose forty-six feet—and this was in a country that rose only two hundred feet in its entire width. The river formed a giant lake that covered much of the interior of the Isthmus. The flow of the water during this flood was nearly eighty thousand cubic feet per second. Anything in the path of this rush downstream was destroyed.[14]

Even if people caught in the jungle during the rainy season could avoid the flooded landscape and torrential currents that formed everywhere, they could not avoid the humidity. Silent and unmoving beneath the forest canopy, the air was always at 100 percent humidity. The air's moisture choked the lungs and ate up everything else. Steel and iron tools and weapons would turn bright orange with rust within a day. Anything made from leather would turn green with mold overnight. Boots and belts would rot completely in a few days. Clothes never dried. It was no wonder the Indians wore no clothes. They did little good. Wherever the ground was not a flowing stream, it was a blue-black muck that grabbed and twisted the feet of those who passed through it. One man saw forty dead mules on the trail into Panama City. Diseases also seemed to come with the rain. Epidemics of yellow fever infected the travelers in 1853 and 1856. Dysentery, cholera, and malaria struck down the men in their tracks.[15]

Bound for California

Despite all the hardships of the passage, thousands of men and women continued to press on across the Isthmus to California and the chance for a prosperous new life. Approximately thirty thousand people crossed Panama in 1852. In 1853 the Hurtado y Hermanos company organized the entire trip across Panama and offered a single fixed price of twenty-five dollars for the boat trip up the Chagres and the mule trip down to Panama City.

Not only were thousands of miners traveling across the Isthmus to reach California, but millions of dollars of the newly found California gold nuggets were traveling the other way, from the Pacific to the Atlantic Ocean, on their way to the United States Mint in Philadelphia to be turned into gold coins. In September 1851 the Pacific Mail Steamship Company's treasure train—seventy or eighty mules loaded with gold nuggets worth $2 million—was attacked seven miles from Panama City. The robbers got away with $250,000 in gold; there were no police to chase down the thieves. Merchants and steamship officials saw the immediate need for a better, more secure passage across the country.[16]

THE PANAMA RAILROAD

Even before gold was discovered in California, businessmen in France and the United States wanted to build a railroad across Panama. In 1845 a French company called the Compagnie de Panama, contracted with the government of New Granada (soon to be renamed Colombia) to build a railroad across the Isthmus and administer it for ninety-nine years. By June 1848, the French company had failed to make a payment on its contract with the government of New Granada and lost its right to build the railroad.

A Railroad Is Needed

Almost immediately—by December of that same year—a company from the United States, the Panama Railroad Company, negotiated a new contract with the government in Bogotá to build the railroad across Panama within six years. Part of this contract stipulated that the railroad company would guarantee a trip across the Isthmus in under twelve hours. No longer would it be a four-day ordeal to survive the Panama jungle. Instead, it would be a pleasant half-day ride on the first transcontinental railroad ever built.[1]

A Railroad Survey Begins

Early in 1849, the directors of the Panama Railroad Company sent a large party of surveyors to Panama to lay out the route for the railroad. These surveyors, under the direction of the chief engineer, Colonel G. W. Hughes, confirmed that the best route across the Isthmus was along the same path that the new miners were using to cross the Isthmus: along the Chagres River to the Continental Divide and then down the Pacific side of the Andes Mountains to Panama City.

This was the same general route that the French surveyors had found several years before. More important, the surveyors from the United States found a low passage over the Continental Divide at Culebra Pass that was only 286 feet above sea level. It would be much easier to build the railroad if it passed through Culebra Pass than if it had to run over the tops of the nearby mountains.

When Edward Sidell returned to New York with the good news from the survey expedition, many people were enthusiastic and wanted to join the project. On June 28, 1849, the Panama Railroad Company began to sell shares in the newly formed company so that it could begin construction. Shares were offered at one hundred dollars each. They planned to raise $1 million. The entire amount was sold by three o'clock in the afternoon.

The railroad company next hired Colonel George M. Totten and John C. Trautwine to direct the construction of the railroad. These two engineers had recently supervised the construction of a canal that joined the Magdalena River to the Atlantic Ocean near Cartagena in New Granada. They were probably the two men most familiar with the problems of working in the jungles of Panama.[2]

How to Build the Railroad?

One of the big problems the engineers faced was finding the materials needed to build the railroad. There was no iron in the entire country—no rails, no engines, not even any nails. Even in the midst of the tangled jungle, there was no supply of harvestable trees that could be used for the ties to lay the tracks. There were no factories. Everything needed for the construction had to be brought by ship from the United States and Europe. Even if they could find the materials from local sources, there were no roads to carry them.

The original plan was first to build the section of the railroad from the Culebra Pass to Panama City. The engineers believed they could use flat-bottomed boats on the Chagres River to ferry the materials they needed from the Atlantic Coast to the construction site. The plan did not work. The boats sent from New York to haul the construction materials sat too deeply in the water, when loaded, to use the Chagres River. Also, it was impossible to hire enough workers since it was both easier and more profitable for the Indians to work as freight carriers or mule drivers for the miners who marched across the Isthmus in a seemingly unending line. In February 1850 the plan was changed and work was started again from Manzanillo Island in Navy Bay on the Atlantic Ocean where supplies could be directly downloaded from the supply ships.[3]

Rails Are Laid

In May 1850, John Trautwine and a few men began clearing the swamps that bordered Manzanillo Island. By July, Colonel Totten had brought nearly one hundred workers from Cartagena and the heavy work of construction began. The engineers and the Indian workers labored side by side, waist deep in the swamp water, often sick from disease, to mark the way and clear the path for the railroad. By December, pile drivers—floating barges that could drive huge logs, called piles, into the swampy bottom of the harbor— arrived from the United States. These piles were used to construct a bridge from the island to firm land at Gatun, more than seven miles away. The first iron rails were laid atop these piles.

The first locomotive arrived and was placed on the rails on June 24, 1851. At first it could not go very far, but by the middle of November the locomotive could travel more than two miles past Gatun.[4] In March 1852 the railroad reached as far as the small village of Bohío Soldado. The Panama Railroad Company announced that daily train departures from Bohío

Soldado to Colón were available. The fare was two dollars for the sixteen-mile trip.[5] By July 1852, twenty-three and a half miles of track were completed from Colón to the Chagres River crossing at Barbacoas, where the river was about three hundred feet wide.

Ulysses S. Grant Comes to Panama

In that same month during the rainy season, seven hundred United States Army troops on their way to California were transported by the railroad to Barbacoas, where they caught the slow riverboats up the Chagres River to Gorgona and Cruces. A captain in charge of a company of these troops was the future president of the United States, Ulysses S. Grant. Many of the men under his command, along with their wives and children, died of cholera on the descent by pack mule into Panama City. "The horrors of the road in the rainy season are beyond description," Grant wrote.[6] Later, when Grant became president, he was fully in favor of constructing the Panama Canal and sent several survey teams to determine the most practical route for it.[7]

Workers on the Railroad

So far, the construction of the railroad had been hard work through the swamps and low-lying jungle, but progress had been constant, as more and more workers from faraway lands had been brought to Panama. Indian workers arrived from New Granada, as well as blacks from Jamaica and Irishmen from New Orleans.

Workers from Jamaica arrive at the dock in Colón ready to go to work in Panama.

Other people came from Philadelphia and New York to work as mechanics. The railroad company sent recruiters to Canton, China, and Ireland. Men came from Germany, France, and Austria.

Once on the job, some deserted because of the unhealthy, hard work. Many others left to go to California and become miners. It was always hard to find workers. By April 1854 there were five thousand men working on the railroad, and a thousand more were needed to finish the work. Most of the men earned eighty cents a day plus their lodging and food. Top mechanics earned a very good salary of between three and four dollars a day.[8]

While building the railroad, there was always the danger of sickness and accidents. The cholera epidemic that swept the Isthmus in 1852 and killed so many in Grant's company also killed forty-eight of the fifty engineers from the United States who were working on the railroad. Hundreds of regular workers also died—many of them unknown and forgotten. It made little difference to the crew leaders if a man died or ran off to California. All they saw was that another replacement was needed. Chinese workers died quickly in the tropical conditions, and many committed suicide in despair.

Horror stories of the terrible working conditions were published in the United States saying that someone died for every railroad tie that was laid down. This was not literally true. There were nearly ninety thousand ties, spaced thirty inches apart, in the finished railroad. Not more than fifteen thousand men ever worked on the railroad. There were other estimates that half the workers died; this might be true. However, no one knows exactly how many men did die in the disease-ridden jungles of Panama. So many died that the hospital for railroad workers in Colón was able to pay its operating expenses by selling the sun-bleached skeletons of unknown workers to medical universities in Europe and the United States.[9]

Despite the deaths, construction of the railroad was progressing on schedule. But two major obstacles remained. The first was to bridge the mighty Chagres River; the second would be to level the hills enough to cross the Continental Divide at Culebra Pass.

The Chagres River

Any bridge over the Chagres would have to be able to withstand its huge floods during the rainy season. It was beyond the powers of the imagination of the engineers to realize just how great a wall of water that could be. The first bridge over the Chagres was almost finished when a sudden rise in the river after a rain swept away an entire span. This disaster postponed the completion of the rails to Gorgona during 1852. A new bridge, 625 feet long and 18 feet wide, was designed to stand 40 feet above the water level during the dry season. Giant blocks of sandstone, quarried from nearby San Pablo, were placed in the riverbed and rose high in the air to support iron girders laid between them. When it was finished it was called one of the longest and finest iron bridges in the world. The first locomotive passed over the new bridge on November 26, 1853, during the height of the rainy season.[10]

Over the Continental Divide

On June 20, 1853, work began on the railroad from the Pacific Ocean. Crews started near the north gate of Panama City and filled in the lowlands and leveled the hills that led north ten miles to the Continental Divide at Culebra Pass. Once this ground was level, ties were put down and iron track laid on top of that. By the end of January 1854, a locomotive and other rolling stock had been brought to the Pacific side and installed on the new track at Panama City. A new work crew of three thousand men was recruited to work on the rails between Obispo and Panama City. Even though the

This is the first Panama Railroad bridge that crossed the Chagres River.

rainy season of 1854 caused mud slides, disease, and desertions, the work continued.

By August 1854, the trains from each side of the Isthmus ran to within a mile of each other. From each side of the Continental Divide the railroad bed rose to meet near the summit. It was planned that the railroad would pass over the summit at Culebra Pass at 250 feet above sea level. In order to make this happen, a channel through the pass—1,300 feet long and 24 feet deep—had to be excavated. An estimated thirty thousand cubic yards of earth had to be removed and dumped as fill along the route. By October the workers excavating from both sides of Culebra Pass were near the summit, within a half mile of each other. The workers on one side could yell encouragement to those on the other side. On October 28, 1854, the Panama Railroad Company advertised trips to the small town of Culebra that was being built at the summit. On a clear day one could stand at Culebra and see both the Atlantic and Pacific oceans.[11]

The Railroad Is Completed

On the evening of January 27, 1855, the last rail of the Panama Railroad was laid. The completed railroad was a tribute to the heroic work of the men who built it—those who hacked away the jungle, filled in the swamps, and laid the rails. The railroad was 47 miles and 3,020 feet long. It started in the man-made harbor of the new city of Colón, on Manzanillo Island in the Atlantic Ocean. It then followed Limón Bay and crossed the Mindi River. It reached the mighty Chagres River at the town of Gatun. It followed the valley of the Chagres and finally crossed the river at Barbacoas and continued to follow it to the Obispo River. The railroad crossed the Continental Divide near the headwaters of the Obispo River and descended the Pacific side into Panama City along the valley of the Rio Grande.[12]

The railroad was a single-track line, with the tracks five feet apart. At first the rails were simple flat iron bars, but these were replaced with wrought iron "U" rails in 1853. These, in turn, were replaced with

This is the Panama Railroad Station at Mamee.

modern steel "upside-down T" rails in 1869. The rails were first laid on pine ties, but these rotted quickly in the tropical climate, and they were replaced, beginning in 1855, with ties made of the very heavy but durable wood, *Lignum vitae,* Latin for the "tree of life."[13]

The ground under the rails was made into a smooth bed that did not rise or descend for more than sixty feet from level in a mile of its length. There were sidings—places to wait for a train from the other direction to pass—at Gatun, Barbacoas, Matachín, and the summit. There were tracks for four trains to park at Aspinwall at the Atlantic terminal and tracks for three trains at Panama City on the Pacific. There were car repair shops, machine shops, and a blacksmith shop in Aspinwall.

The railroad had six heavy and four light locomotives and twenty-two passenger cars, each of which could seat sixty passengers. There were fifty-one freight cars and seventy-two platform cars. Wood, which was burned to create the steam that powered the locomotives, was sold along the route for three dollars a cord. The cost of the railroad, including all the rolling stock, land, and other expenses was $6,564,552.95.[14]

First Passage

The day after the last rail was laid, January 28, 1855, a steam engine made the first passage from the Atlantic to the Pacific Ocean. The first transcontinental railroad was born. For a few weeks, there were delays

This is the terminus of the Panama Railroad, the world's first transcontinental railroad, at Panama City.

on the passages as mud slides from late rains covered the tracks, and crews of workers had to shovel the way clear. But on February 15, the Panama Railroad Company fulfilled the terms of its contract to make the journey in twelve hours; it completed the trip in just four and a half hours.[15]

Matthew Fontaine Maury, the leading United States government scientist and geographer of the time, wrote to Congress in 1849:

> The railroad across the Isthmus of Panama will speedily lead to the construction of a ship canal between the two oceans, for a railroad can not do the business which commerce will require for it; and by showing to the world how immense this business is, men will come from the four [corners of the world] to urge with purse and tongue the construction of a ship canal.[16]

Maury was right. During the first ten years of the railroad's operation, from 1856 to 1866, a total of 396,032 people crossed the Isthmus of Panama on its rails.[17] The cost to ride those forty-seven miles—twenty-five dollars in gold—made it the world's most expensive train ride. But travelers thought the ride was well worth it. On the way to the Atlantic Coast of the United States, the railroad carried $501,218,748 in gold and $147,377,113 in silver safely across the continent. In the first six years after the railroad was completed, the profits to the railroad company totaled more than $7 million. Shares in the Panama Railroad Company rose to become the most expensive stock on the New York Stock Market at $295 a share in June 1869.[18]

The railroad also carried approximately 614,535 tons of mail, baggage, merchandise, and coal from ocean to ocean during those ten years. This seems like a lot, but it was only a tiny amount in comparison to the vast amount of material needed in California to build the new cities and factories that would support

Nearly four hundred thousand people rode the rails across the Isthmus of Panama during the first ten years of the railroad's operation.

the hundreds of thousands of new immigrants from around the world.

Freight charges were quite expensive on the railroad. Passenger baggage cost between ten and fifteen cents a pound. Express freight and merchandise was charged $1.80 per cubic foot. Only the lightest and most costly material bound for California could bear such an expense. Most of the heavy freight that was bound for California from the rest of the United

States and Europe still made the long, slow, dangerous voyage around the tip of South America. Very soon, it was not fast or good enough. In 1865, Matthew Fontaine Maury's words of 1849 came true as men from around the world began to arrive to build the Panama Canal.

5

THE FRENCH CANAL

The Suez Canal extends more than 105 miles across the desert sands of Egypt's Suez Peninsula. It is a simple channel in the earth, constructed completely at sea level. In 1869 the Suez Canal opened with a procession of more than fifty ships, including the royal yachts of France and Austria-Hungary. It allowed ships to travel between Europe and the great Asian markets in China, Japan, and India without traveling around the continent of Africa. The canal immediately became a great business success. Ferdinand de Lesseps, the man who supervised its construction, became the most famous man in Europe, known as the Great Frenchman and the Great Engineer.[1]

De Lesseps and the Panama Canal

Ferdinand de Lesseps became interested in building another interoceanic canal, this time across the Isthmus of Panama. He joined several French businessmen to form a private company with an impressive name: the Société Civile Internationale du Canal Interocéanique du Darien. The Société sent

*The great success of the Suez Canal, shown here, inspired
the French to begin building a canal across Panama.*

Lucien Napoleon-Bonaparte Wyse, a grandnephew of
the first French emperor, Napoleon Bonaparte, to
Panama in early November 1876, to survey the site for
a canal and, more important, to secure the permission
of the country of New Granada for such a project.

Once in Panama, Lucien Wyse made a dangerous
and exciting trip through the jungle to Bogotá, the
capital of New Granada, eighty-six hundred feet high
in the Andes Mountains. He had an interview with the
officers of the New Granada government and they
came to an agreement. For an initial payment of nearly
two hundred thousand dollars as well as a yearly rental
fee, the Société was granted permission to build and

administer a canal for ninety-nine years. In order to build the canal, New Granada gave to the Société a belt of land 200 meters (219 yards) wide across the entire width of Panama. At the end of ninety-nine years, the canal and the land would be returned to New Granada. Wyse left Bogotá and returned to Panama.

In 1873 the United States government had conducted surveys of a potential canal route across Panama but had rejected it as unsuitable. Wyse never conducted a survey of the canal route himself. He took an easy way out to save some time and a lot of discomfort. He decided to use the notes of the United States survey instead.[2] Wyse sold the supplies he had brought, gave away his surveying tools to a local Panamanian engineer, and left Panama for home to report to de Lesseps.

The French Plan

The French plan for the canal was quite simple. They would cut a sixty-mile-long channel across the Isthmus at sea level. They would follow a route that ran close to the existing Panama Railroad. They planned to use the railroad to transport supplies and haul away the excavated dirt. Once the excavation had reached sea level, the canal itself would be dug another twenty-seven and a half feet deep. The canal would be seventy-two feet wide at its bottom. They planned to complete the canal in twelve years.[3]

Problems with the Plan

The idea of this sea-level canal proved impossible to achieve. The Chagres River valley in Panama, through which any canal would have to go, stood at an altitude of eighty to one hundred feet above sea level. Every year during the rainy season, the Chagres overflowed its banks and flooded most of the valley. That flood of water would pour down in a spectacular waterfall into any sea-level canal that was dug through the valley. It would then flow in both directions into the oceans at either end of the canal, carrying any ships on the canal at that time to certain destruction.

No one ever took this problem seriously. De Lesseps simply said that it was indeed a problem, but that they should not worry. In all great projects, like the construction of the Suez Canal, he told them, enormous problems arose. Always, a man would rise up with the right solution. Since it was the hero of Suez, the Great Engineer, who told them this, most people simply accepted his word.

Even if they could divert the waters of the Chagres River, the huge size of the hole that would have to be dug across Panama made a sea-level canal seem fantastic. Many miles of the interior plateau that rose to nearly one hundred feet along the route would have to be dug away to create a level path two hundred feet wide before they could even dig the canal itself.[4]

An international conference of engineers was called by the Société in May 1879 to gain support for the French Canal venture, and an alternative plan was presented by the delegates from the United States. The American plan was based on the idea that it would be much easier to raise the ships on the canal up the mountainside, rather than dig the mountainside away beneath them. Locks were the steps that ships could use to climb a mountain.

Canal Locks

Locks work to raise a ship in much the same way that toys floating in a bathtub will rise as the tub is filled with water. Two massive sets of doors are placed in the canal channel wide enough apart to accommodate the largest ship designed to pass through the canal. One set of the doors, at the upper side of the passage, is closed to prevent the waters on the higher side of the canal from flowing downhill. The other set of doors is open and holds water at the lower level. A ship enters the lock and the lower-level doors are closed behind it. Water is then allowed to flow into the lock, and the ship rises as the water level rises, just as a toy in the bathtub rises as the tub fills. When the water level in the lock is the same as the upper level of the canal, the upper-level doors are opened and the ship passes through the lock and into the upper level. With both doors closed, the water in the lock is allowed to flow out of the lock until the lower level is again reached. The lower-level doors are then opened and the lock is ready for another ship. By a series of such locks, a ship can be raised to an enormous height and then lowered again.[5]

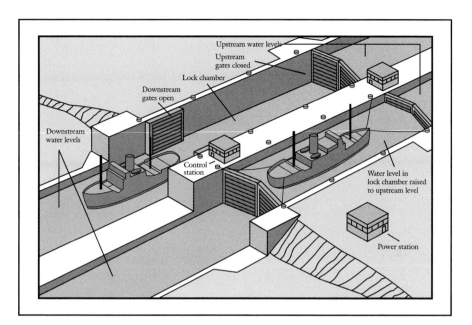

Upstream water level

Upstream gates closed

Lock chamber

Downstream gates open

Downstream water levels

Control station

Water level in lock chamber raised to upstream level

Power station

The process of moving a ship through locks is much like filling a bathtub with water. Whatever is floating on the water is lifted to the level at which the water stops.

The American plan called for twelve locks on each side of the Continental Divide to raise ships 124 feet into the air from sea level. At that height, construction of a long stone canal built through the Continental Divide linking the Atlantic side and Pacific side locks would be necessary.

It was this plan that the government of the United States had rejected. It decided to try to build a canal across Nicaragua instead. De Lesseps was opposed to any canal across Panama that used locks. He had completed the Suez Canal successfully without locks, and he was determined to construct the Panama Canal in the same way. Both the United States government and Ferdinand de Lesseps were correct to reject this proposal because it ignored the same problem as the original sea-level canal—the rain and the Chagres River floods.

Another Idea: Lakes

At the conference, there was a third proposal for the design of the Panama Canal. Baron Godin de Lépinay had been an engineer for the French company that had built the Mexican railroad from Córdoba to Veracruz in 1862. The baron's plan called for the construction of two large lakes, one on each side of the Continental Divide. The lake on the Pacific side would be created by the construction of a dam on the waters of the Rio Grande. On the Atlantic side of the mountains, another lake would be formed by damming the waters of the Chagres River. Both dams would be designed to keep the lake levels at the same height of eighty feet above sea level. The baron's plan then called for the excavation of a channel between the two lakes for the ships to pass over the Continental Divide at Culebra Pass. This would be the only excavation that was needed. To reach the level of the lakes at eighty feet, there would be a set of three locks on each side of the canal.

This was a brilliant proposal in many ways. It would be quicker and less expensive to construct than any other kind of canal. It not only saved over eighty feet of excavation through miles of the Panama jungle plateau, but also solved the problem of the flooding Chagres River. Instead of fighting nature in what would be a losing battle to control the massive rainfall, the baron's plan would use all that excess water to create a massive lake that was designed to be a working part of the canal. They could use the water of the lake to power the locks by simply allowing the water to flow downhill through the locks.

Like many brilliant ideas, this plan was dismissed as ridiculous. Ferdinand de Lesseps had made up his mind that he wanted a sea-level canal—a mistake that would cost tens of thousands of lives and millions of dollars. The conference voted in support of de Lesseps's plan to build the canal in twelve years for a cost of $214 million.[6]

Work Gets Started

Work on the French Canal was slow to get started. Most of 1881 was spent gaining control of the Panama Railroad and moving supplies and equipment to Panama. The first workers on the canal were forty French engineers under the direction of Gaston Blanchet, the chief engineer. It was their job to lay out the exact route of the canal.

They arrived in January 1881 and hired crews of local workers to do the hard labor of cutting away the jungle. By summer there were two hundred French engineers and more than eight hundred local laborers working together. They continued to hack away at the jungle during the rainy season, and before they reached the Continental Divide, they had crossed the Chagres River fourteen times.

By the end of 1881, there were two thousand men working on the canal. Workers came from Colombia, Venezuela, and Cuba, but the majority of the new workers were recruited from Jamaica and the United States. The next year, there were four thousand men at work. By September 1883 there were ten thousand workers; by October 1884 there were nineteen thou sand men digging the trench across the country.[7]

The laborers worked with the usual hand tools—axes, picks, shovels, and wheelbarrows. Lengths of the canal along the drier areas were dug by crews of laborers with only these tools. The work did not proceed smoothly, and little was accomplished during the dry season of 1882. When the rains came, most work stopped.

The crews working on the excavations of the higher lands near the Continental Divide used three steam shovels, as well as picks and hand shovels, to dig away the mountainside. In the low-lying swampy regions near the coasts, dredges would dip into the marsh and dig a channel through the mud. Every year the rains came. In June 1884, thirteen inches of rain fell at the Culebra Pass; in August, there were sixteen inches, in September, ten inches, in October, twenty-two inches. With the rain came mud. The mud would not only stop the work, but also fill in whatever channels had been dug that year with mountains of mud.[8]

The base of the Culebra Pass was made of a blue clay—"a clay that is utterly impossible for a man to throw off his shovel once he gets it on. He had to have

This is one of the dredges used during the French effort to construct a canal across Panama.

a little scraper to shove it off."[9] On top of that clay was what geologists called the Cucaracha or the "cockroach," formation, hundreds of feet of mixed lava flow muds, shales, gravel, and just plain dirt. Every year during the rainy season, the Cucaracha would slide downhill over the underlying slippery blue clay into the newly dug excavation that the canal builders had taken the entire dry season to empty.[10]

Big Problems

In June 1884, a United States naval officer, Lieutenant Robert Brown, sent a secret report to the secretary of the Navy stating that only one thirtieth of the work had been completed on the canal, although about half of the original time estimate to complete the canal had expired. The report also commented that more than half of all the money to construct the canal had already been spent. Brown declared that "the completion of this Canal, according to present plans, is very doubtful. It certainly will require much more time and money than originally estimated."[11]

Another independent evaluation of the French effort, this time by a British naval officer, Captain Bedford Pim, in October 1884, concluded: "It appears that the physical obstacles are insurmountable while the financial difficulties are scarcely less, although it is not yet too late to build a canal with locks." He went on to say: "Every credit, not to say praise, has been given to the gallant employees who have struggled manfully to carry out the wishes of their chief, Mons. de Lesseps."[12]

Pim was certainly correct. The heroism and dedication of the workers on the French Panama Canal cannot be adequately stated. During that first rainy season of work in 1881, men began to die. Several cases of yellow fever among the local laborers were reported in May. The first worker died in the second week of June. On July 25, a French engineer died of a fever. On July 28, Henri Bionne, another French engineer who had been in Panama less than two weeks, met the same fate. That summer, ten of the twenty men in one surveying party died suddenly from disease. One of the men, a Russian named Dziembowski (his first name has been lost to historians), feeling fine, bought a new suit of clothes one morning and was buried in it at dawn the next day. He had died of yellow fever. In November, Gaston Blanchet, the chief engineer for the canal, died of malaria.[13]

Disease Strikes

There were at least two epidemics that ravaged Panama and the canal workers at the same time, yellow fever and malaria. No one at the time knew how they came or how they spread.

Yellow fever was truly frightening. More than half the people who caught yellow fever died. The attack began with fits of shivering, high fever, and a thirst that no amount of water could quench. The body of the sufferer would ache all over with pain and severe headaches, and soon the face and the eyes would turn yellow. After a day or so of this restless torment, the patient would begin to vomit mouthfuls of dark blood in fits that would make the body squirm on the floor. The vomiting would stop and then, more than half the time, the body, exhausted and empty, would grow cold and die. Yellow fever would kill many people for a time and then it would seem to go away. It would always return with the rains.

No one knew how yellow fever came and went in Panama, but everyone knew that malaria, the other great epidemic, was always present. Malaria, like yellow fever, began with uncontrollable fits of shivering, chills, and chattering teeth. A high fever and terrible thirst followed quickly. If the patient did not die of this fever in its first attack, malaria could and often did return to attack again and again. The canal workers knew that high doses of quinine, a powder made from the bark of the cinchona tree of South America, would prevent its symptoms. The French freely distributed it, but it tasted horrible and many took too little or failed to take it often enough. More people probably died from malaria than from yellow fever in Panama.[14]

The canal company built a 200-bed hospital in Colón and another at Ancon near Panama City. The hospitals were staffed by nurses from the Sisters of St. Vincent de Paul Society in France. Of the people who entered those hospitals, 75 percent died there. Only two of the first twenty-four nurses survived.

In 1883, an estimated thirteen hundred died from epidemic diseases, more than 10 percent of all the workers on the canal at that time. In later years it became worse; it is estimated that 20 percent of the workers on the canal died each year.[15] Many never reached the hospital or a cemetery. So many died in the camps that bodies were simply gathered in the morning and buried. No record was ever kept of who died when, or what happened to the body.

Chief Engineer Jules Dingler brought his family to Panama in the fall of 1883. In January 1884, his daughter, about eighteen years old, caught yellow fever and died. In February, his son also caught the disease and died. On New Year's Eve, his wife died. Dingler resigned and returned to France, a man with a broken

Thousands of people died during the years of work on the French Canal. This view is of the French cemetery at Ancon, near Panama City, where many of the victims of disease were buried.

spirit.[16] Dingler's replacement as chief engineer, Maurice Hutin, came down with yellow fever, survived it, and returned to France. His replacement, Philippe Bunau-Varilla, also caught yellow fever, but survived and resigned. The next replacement, Léon Boyer, died from yellow fever. The French newspapers never spoke of the casualties, but everyone in France knew that going to Panama was suicide. The French graduates of fine engineering schools knew that they were probably going to die in Panama, but they applied for the jobs by the hundreds.[17] These new engineers ignored the dangers, seeing only the opportunities for quickly won fame and advancement. They were inspired to devote themselves to the project for the glory of France.

A New Chief Engineer

Philippe Bunau-Varilla, a young engineering graduate, when asked why he wanted to go to Panama, replied, "As an officer runs to it when he hastens to the battlefield, and not as the coward who flees from the sorrows of life."[18] Bunau-Varilla became the chief engineer of the entire canal project at the age of twenty-six in August 1885. He wrote that the discomforts and the dangers of the work in Panama "exalted the energy of those who were filled with a sincere love for the great task undertaken. To its irradiating influence was joined the heroic joy of self-sacrifice for the greatness of France."[19]

It was a war—a war against the jungle. Philippe Bunau-Varilla spoke for his generation. The young men of France who enlisted to go to Panama were inspired by that patriotic fervor, and they died by the thousands in a battle against an unseen enemy.

When Bunau-Varilla became the director of the canal project in 1885, only about one tenth of the estimated total of 150 million cubic yards of material had been removed to dig the sea-level canal. More large machinery was needed. Too much was still being done by hand. There were never enough well-trained workers. If an adequately trained worker did not die of disease, he would quit and return home as soon as he could. Any new workers had to be trained to replace him.

It was usually reported by the inspectors who visited the project that even more time and money would be needed to complete the canal than the last time they had visited Panama. But it was also usually reported that the French would eventually succeed. As always, two major problems remained unsolved: the Culebra Cut and the Chagres River. Bunau-Varilla estimated that 25 million cubic yards of rock had to be dug out of the mountainside of the Continental Divide on a line over a mile and a half long. He worked at the problem from both ends of the cut and finally increased the excavation to 1.4 million cubic yards a month in January 1886. It made little difference. As soon as the rains began, the cut filled with mud slides again. It looked as if the entire canal could be dug except for the cut through the mountains. The French never addressed the problem of the Chagres River.[20] They ignored it. They never made plans for the dam they said was needed to hold back the floodwaters. They never even found a place to quarry the stone that would be needed to build it. They simply did not talk about it.

Bankruptcy

There was always a need for more money. Despite the efforts of Ferdinand de Lesseps, the canal company eventually went bankrupt. On February 4, 1889, the canal company was dissolved by the French courts. Work on the canal continued until May 15, 1889, at which time the project was abandoned. Dredges were left where they floated. The excavators, locomotives, and railroad cars were moved onto sidings and left, exposed to the weather. The hospitals closed. The villages were deserted. The workers sailed for home. The partially completed sections of the vast trench across Panama were gradually filled in with the luxurious growth of the jungle. Soon it was hard to tell that the land there had ever been naked and scarred, touched by man. More than eight hundred thousand Frenchmen lost their investment in the canal. Many lost not only their families' entire savings, but also the lives of their sons, who had disappeared in the jungle.[21]

The bankers who oversaw the dissolution of the French Canal Company just abandoned the heavy earth-moving equipment found along the route. It was not worth the cost of moving it. There were other assets of the French company, however, that were still valuable.

THE UNITED STATES IN PANAMA

A New French Effort

The most valuable asset was the rights the canal company had negotiated with the government of Colombia. (The country formerly known as New Granada had become the Republic of Colombia in 1886.) The bankers reorganized and began business as the Compagnie Nouvelle du Canal de Panama; the new company formally incorporated on October 20, 1894. They sent an emissary to Bogotá, Colombia, who negotiated a series of two-year extensions to the old contract. They sent a small crew of engineers to Panama and completed new plans for the lock canal that was based primarily on the model proposed by Godin de Lépinay in 1879. They maintained the buildings and docks. They operated the Panama Railroad. They did just enough excavation to fulfill their contracts with Colombia. They were just waiting. They planned to sell the whole thing to the United States.[1]

The United States Gets Involved

The directors of the new French company were patient. The Spanish-American War in 1898 had revealed the need for an interoceanic canal for the ships of the United States Navy. Philippe Bunau-Varilla visited the United States and sought business and governmental approval for the purchase of the French company in Panama.

The new young president, Theodore Roosevelt, wanted an Isthmus canal and he developed support for the idea in Congress. The United States government arranged a treaty with the Colombian ambassador to Washington, D.C., Tomás Herrán, that gave the United States the right to build a canal. Roosevelt then used his influence to see that the United States Senate, which must approve all foreign treaties, approved this one, the Hay-Herrán Treaty. The treaty won a hard-fought approval in the Senate, but the government of Colombia rejected it unanimously in 1903. The United States intended to pay $40 million directly to France for its interest in the canal holdings. When it became apparent to the government of Colombia that none of the money would be paid directly to Colombia for the overdue debts of the French canal company, they rejected the treaty. They wanted guarantees that the French would pay their debts.[2]

The Country of Panama Is Born

Despite this setback, the United States, especially President Theodore Roosevelt, was determined to have an interoceanic canal across the province of Panama regardless of how the country of Colombia felt about it. A group of Panamanians, who were also interested in the completion of a canal across their land, and Frenchman Philippe Bunau-Varilla came to the United States and secured government approval and support for a declaration of independence of Panama as a new country, separate from Colombia.

On November 3, 1903, the rebels launched their coup—an attempt to overthrow the government—in Panama City. General Esteban Huertas was the commander of the local army detachment. He was young and ambitious. He sided with the rebels for the new country. At four in the afternoon, Huertas led some of his loyal troops and arrested the visiting Colombian Army officers who happened to be inspecting the harbor defenses at the time. They were marched to the square and placed in the jail. An irrevocable step had been taken. The only other troops loyal to Colombia were across the Isthmus at Colón on the Atlantic Ocean side. The presence of the U.S.S. *Nashville*, ready at a battle station in the harbor, and the expected arrival of the U.S.S. *Dixie* with six thousand United States Army troops convinced Colonel Elisio Torres, commander of the visiting Colombian officers, to take his troops and depart Panama forever aboard a British mail steamer, H.M.S.

WHITE HOUSE,
 WASHINGTON.

PERSONAL

Oyster Bay, N.Y.,
September 15, 1903.

Dear John:

I entirely approve of your idea. Let us do nothing in the
Colombia matter at present. I shall be back in Washington by
the 28th instant, and you a week or two afterwards. Then we
will go over the matter very carefully and decide what to do.
At present I feel that there are two alternatives. (1) To
take up Nicaragua; (2) in some shape or way to interfere when
it becomes necessary so as to secure the Panama route without
further dealing with the foolish and homicidal corruptionists
in Bogota. I am not inclined to have any further dealings
whatever with those Bogota people.

Faithfully yours,

Theodore Roosevelt

Hon. John Hay,
 Secretary of State.

President Theodore Roosevelt was very interested in an American effort to build a canal through Panama. In this letter, he discusses the issue of the canal with his secretary of state, John Hay.

Orinoco. The new country of Panama, about the size of the state of South Carolina, had a population of about three hundred fifty thousand.[3]

A Treaty

Less than two weeks later, on November 18, 1903, the United States concluded the negotiations for a canal treaty with the new country of Panama. John Hay, the secretary of state, signed a treaty with Philippe Bunau-Varilla that radically changed the former agreement the United States had with the government of Colombia. Philippe Bunau-Varilla was in no way an official of any government. He was a French citizen living in Panama at the time. It was an illegal agreement. It was written by the two men to be so advantageous to the United States that it would immediately get the support of the Senate, which had to approve the final treaty.

This new Hay-Bunau-Varilla Treaty simply gave the United States ownership of the ten-mile-wide strip of land across the country that would contain the canal. And it gave ownership to the United States forever. For this, the United States government would pay Panama the same amount that it would have paid Colombia—$10 million. The new government of Panama formally approved the treaty on December 2, 1903. On February 23, 1904, the United States Senate approved the treaty by a vote of 66 to 14.[4]

The reaction to the United States from Colombia and other countries in Latin America was outrage. It was perceived by many that the United States had simply stolen what it had wanted from a weaker neighbor. As one United States minister said in 1912:

> The confidence and trust in the justice and fairness of the United States, so long manifested, has completely vanished, and the maleficent influence of this condition is permeating public opinion in all Latin-American countries, a condition which, if remedial measures are not invoked, will work inestimable harm throughout the Western Hemisphere.[5]

Buying the Rights to Build the Canal

On May 4, 1904, the United States bought the French Canal company and all its assets for $40 million. It was the largest check that the United States had ever written. The United States had paid more for the old French Canal than it had for the entire Louisiana Purchase, Alaska, and the Philippines combined.[6] On May 9, 1904, President Roosevelt placed the newly created Canal Zone under the direction of the War Department. Major General George W. Davis was appointed to be the Zone's first governor. John Findlay Wallace was appointed the chief engineer. When Wallace and his wife arrived in the Canal Zone, they brought along two fine metal caskets as part of their luggage.[7] It was obvious that the first and foremost problem on the Isthmus was still the threat of disease, and people were well aware that death could be part of the bargain if they chose to move to Panama.

Disease Threatens the Americans

In the years since the end of the French Canal effort, scientists had discovered that mosquitoes were the mysterious vehicle for the transmission of both malaria and yellow fever. These deadly diseases were caused by one-celled organisms called protozoa. A female mosquito would bite a person infected with yellow fever or malaria and suck up the protozoa along with blood during the bite. The protozoa would grow and reproduce inside the stomach of the mosquito. The infected mosquito would then spread the protozoa to other humans when it bit them. It was also learned that only one mosquito species, the *Stegomyia fasciata*, carried yellow fever. The *Stegomyia* mosquito was quite delicate; it could not fly very far and it needed human blood in order to reproduce. The females of this particular species of mosquito also needed pools of clean water to deposit their tiny black eggs. Simply by covering the containers of fresh water and draining stagnant pools of rainwater, it was possible to deprive the female mosquito of a chance to reproduce. The life cycle of the mature mosquito is short, three to four weeks, so without breeding grounds, this deadly species of mosquito could be controlled by following a few simple rules of cleanliness around areas inhabited by humans.

Malaria, the other deadly disease in Panama, was also spread by the bite of a mosquito. The life cycle of the disease was the same as yellow fever. The culprit was a protozoa of the genus *Plasmodium,* which grew inside the stomach of the mosquito. In the case of malaria, it was the mosquitoes of the genus *Anopheles* and the disease was transmitted to the victim in the saliva of the bite. The *Anopheles* mosquito is much harder to eradicate than *Stegomyia* since *Anopheles* can deposit its eggs in any pool of stagnant water, clean or dirty. *Anopheles* can also fly much farther than *Stegomyia*. It can live and breed in the jungle away from any human controls and then fly long distances to bite and infect its human victims. Malaria was never controlled.

Colonel William C. Gorgas, an army doctor who had reduced the number of yellow fever cases in Havana, Cuba, in 1901 to zero from over fourteen hundred the year before, was selected to be the chief

sanitary officer for the new Canal Zone. When Gorgas first arrived on April 5, 1904, he found mosquitoes everywhere. After dark in the wards of the local hospitals, mosquitoes were so thick in the air that nurses had to

William C. Gorgas worked hard to eliminate yellow fever in the Canal Zone.

use fans to keep them off the doctors and patients. Gorgas immediately put to use methods that had proved successful in Havana. He put up screens on the windows and doors of homes and hospitals; he cleaned away garbage and refuse lying about in the streets and vacant lots; he drained stagnant pools of water; he covered the pots of drinking water with lids; and he fumigated buildings by burning sulfur to kill adult mosquitoes.[8]

The efforts of the United States medical services in Panama were extensive and effective. Still, they never completely conquered the jungle diseases. Hospital records show that 5,609 men died of diseases and accidents in the ten years of American Canal construction, more than one per day. In all, including the deaths during the French construction efforts, more than twenty-five thousand men died. In other words, approximately five hundred lives ended for each mile of the finished canal.[9]

A New Chief Engineer

John F. Stevens replaced John Wallace as the chief engineer of the canal in July 1905. Stevens was the perfect man for the job. He was a strong, rugged man, who remained calm in the face of troubles. He believed that hard work was the key to success. He had worked building over a thousand miles of railroad track in Mexico, British Columbia, and the United States.[10]

The most important job that Stevens found when he first arrived in Panama was to provide adequate housing and food for the workers. There were few farms in Panama to feed the approximately seventeen thousand new workers coming to work on the canal. Meat was almost nonexistent, the price of fresh fish was high, and a dozen eggs cost a full day's wages. Stevens had a cold storage plant constructed at Colón and refrigeration cars built for the Panama Railroad. Soon, frozen food was being shipped from New York and delivered to fifteen towns across the Isthmus every day. There, the food was prepared in restaurants and sold to the workers for thirty cents a meal. Housing for nearly three quarters of the workers was constructed at these sites.[11]

Stevens tried to make living conditions more bearable for the American construction team on the Panama Canal, with such features as post offices. The first United States post office in Panama, built in 1904, is shown here.

This is the first United States schoolhouse in Panama, built at Gorgona in 1904. Education was provided free to the families of canal employees.

Living conditions in the Canal Zone improved dramatically. Barracks for the workers were constructed. At first, there were no places except bars for the workers to relax after work. Stevens had club rooms with facilities for billiards, bowling, cards, reading, and smoking constructed at Cristóbal, Gorgona, Empire, and Culebra. The streets of Panama City and Colón were paved. Sewer and freshwater systems were installed in 1905 and 1906. On January 17, 1907, electricity first illuminated the homes at Culebra.[12]

Construction of the Canal

The new chief engineer then turned his attention to the construction of the canal itself. Stevens was firmly convinced that a lock canal was the only possible solution to the problem of the Culebra Cut. At the request of President Roosevelt, he traveled to Washington, D.C., and helped convince Congress to insist that any United States government money be spent on a lock, not a sea-level, canal.

When Stevens returned to Panama, he turned to the work at the Culebra Cut. Here, a passage would have to be cut through the mountains so that the channel through which the water flowed would be at an altitude of eighty-five feet. He made big changes quickly. He built over forty miles of new railroad track, ordered large flatcars and locomotives to haul away the excavated material from the cut, strengthened the bridges, and installed an eight-mile-long air line to run tools powered by compressed air. Most important, Stevens restored morale to the men along the canal route. He worked hard in all kinds of weather, he spoke with and encouraged the men, but most of all he did whatever he promised. The workers began to expect to succeed. In their minds, they could see the finished canal.[13]

Since the time of the French Canal effort, there had been great improvements in the performance and size of steam-powered machines. In November 1904, new ninety-five-ton Bucyrus steam shovels manufactured in Milwaukee, Wisconsin, were installed in the Culebra Cut. They were three times larger than the machines that had been used by the French. Soon there were twenty-three of these mammoth shovels that could take roughly eight tons—or five cubic yards—of earth and rock in one scoop at work on the Culebra Cut.

First, holes were drilled and filled with dynamite in the area that was to be removed from the cut. After the dynamite had been set off, the massive steam shovels were moved in to remove the broken rock and rubble. Each machine would work an area fifty feet wide and twelve feet deep. One machine could load a railroad car in eight minutes. Each machine required a crew of ten men to operate it. There was an engineer to move the entire machine and another to operate the shovel. Two men fed the massive boiler that generated the steam, and six men leveled the ground for the steam shovel to move into position. The steam shovel engineers earned $210 a month, as much as the highest paid office workers of the canal.[14]

The workers who operated these machines came from countries around the world, and they often lived on their equipment. On one shovel, the chief engineer was an Irishman, the crane operator was from the United States, two Jamaicans stoked the fires, and six Sikhs from India worked on the ground. The shovels normally worked eight hours a day from seven to eleven in the morning and from one to five in the afternoon. By early 1908, these shovels were removing more than 1.25 million cubic yards each month. The excavation at Culebra became the largest man-made hole in the history of the world.[15]

With the final decision to build the lock canal, it was obvious that the level of the water in the lake, formed by the dam of the Chagres River, would have to be eighty-five feet above sea level, the same as the level of the Culebra Cut. With that final objective in view, plans for the dam were drawn up. The dam was placed at Gatun near the Atlantic Ocean, where the Chagres River ran through a narrow valley between two rock formations. It would be a massive dam, and the lake that formed behind it would also be huge. When the dam was completed, 163.38 square miles of land would be flooded.

About six-thirty each morning, sixty locomotives would pull out of the train yards on the Atlantic and Pacific sides of the Culebra Cut, each coupled to twenty to thirty flatcars. They would spend the day making

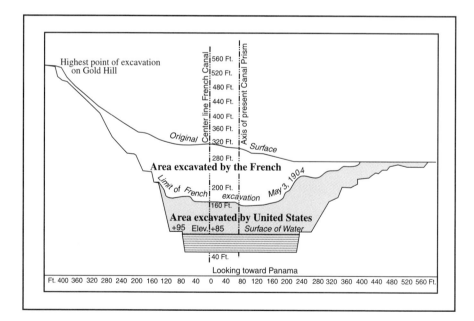

This is a comparative diagram of the French and United States efforts to dig the Culebra Cut.

innumerable trips from the cut to the construction site of the dam. When a loaded train reached the dam construction site, it was immediately unloaded by a large plowshare, a three-ton steel blade called a Lidgerwood unloader, that was pulled through all of the loaded flatcars by a steam-operated drum behind the locomotive. The Lidgerwood unloader finished unloading twenty flatcars in ten minutes. One machine could do the work of three hundred men. Once the now empty train was on its way back to the cut for more, another machine, called the spreader, which was powered by a locomotive and had large plowshares that could open and close, pushed through the rubble and moved it away from the tracks. When that area of the dam site was filled, another machine moved the railroad tracks so that the job could continue.[16] With such a coordinated and steam-powered effort, tremendous progress could be seen toward the completed canal.

7

THE UNITED STATES COMPLETES THE CANAL

On November 14, 1906, the president of the United States, Theodore Roosevelt, arrived at Limón Bay on the battleship U.S.S. *Louisiana* for a three-day tour of the Canal Zone. In three hectic days during the height of the rainy season, Roosevelt went everywhere. He visited the hospitals, lunched with several hundred men at a Canal Zone restaurant, sat in a working Bucyrus steam shovel in the Culebra Cut, inspected the living quarters of the workers, made speeches, and talked to anyone who approached him. He was pleased by what he saw.[1] At the end of his visit, Roosevelt reported to Congress: "It is a stupendous work upon which our fellow countrymen are engaged in down there on the Isthmus. . . . No man can see these young, vigorous men energetically doing their duty without a thrill of pride."[2]

The Work Continues

And, indeed, it was work for young men. John Stevens, the chief engineer, was fifty-five years old in 1907. He usually worked fourteen hours each day,

President Theodore Roosevelt (at center in white suit) sits in a ninety-five-ton Bucyrus steam shovel during a visit to the canal in November 1906.

NOW WE HAVE TAKEN HOLD OF THE JOB. WE HAVE DIFFICULTIES WITH OUR OWN PEOPLE, OF COURSE. I HAVEN'T A DOUBT THAT IT WILL TAKE A LITTLE LONGER AND COST A LITTLE MORE THAN MEN NOW APPRECIATE, BUT I BELIEVE THAT THE WORK IS BEING DONE WITH A VERY HIGH DEGREE BOTH OF EFFICIENCY AND HONESTY; AND I AM IMMENSELY STRUCK BY THE CHARACTER OF AMERICAN EMPLOYEES WHO ARE ENGAGED NOT MERELY IN SUPERINTENDING THE WORK, BUT IN DOING ALL THE JOBS THAT NEED SKILL AND INTELLIGENCE. THE STEAM SHOVELS, DIRT TRAINS, THE MACHINE SHOPS, AND THE LIKE ARE ALL FILLED WITH AMERICAN ENGINEERS, CONDUCTORS, MACHINISTS, BOILERMAKERS, CARPENTERS. FROM THE TOP TO THE BOTTOM THESE MEN ARE SO HARDY, SO EFFICIENT, SO ENERGETIC, THAT IT IS A REAL PLEASURE TO LOOK AT THEM.[3]

This is an excerpt from a letter President Theodore Roosevelt wrote to his son, Kermit, during a trip he made to Panama to inspect the progress on the building of the canal.

supervising the canal construction. After more than two years, he was tired of the constant work and concentration. He resigned his position on March 31, 1907. Stevens was well liked by the construction workers at the canal. Over ten thousand workers signed a petition asking him to reconsider and remain as their boss. When he refused, the workers bought him a gold watch and a diamond ring as retirement presents. He had done a fine job organizing the canal work. His mechanized system of excavating the Culebra Cut and building the Gatun Dam with the rubble would be followed until the canal was completed. The work was progressing well. Over five hundred thousand cubic yards had been removed from Culebra that January. President Roosevelt soon appointed someone who could not quit— a United States Army officer, Major George Washington Goethals—to be the chief engineer.[4]

Major George Washington Goethals took over as chief engineer on the Panama Canal in 1907.

Yet Another New Chief Engineer

Major Goethals, like John Stevens, worked long and hard. He lived at Culebra. Every morning he had breakfast at 6:30. He then caught either the northbound train at 7:10 or the southbound at 7:19 to inspect the work along the route of the canal. He returned to Culebra at noon. After a light lunch, he worked in his office until 7:00 P.M. After supper, he would return to the office and work until 10:00 or 11:00 P.M.[5]

By February 1, 1909, the first five miles on the Pacific side of the Panama Canal were completed and two mail steamers with whistles blowing entered the channel to the cheers of onlookers. The work on the sea-level excavation on the Atlantic side of the Continental Divide was also progressing on schedule. Major Goethals was equally impressed with the work at Culebra and at Gatun, and he determined to make no changes in the efficient system. He saw, however, that a great deal needed to be done to construct the locks. Only the preliminary clearing of the land and the basic designs had been completed when he became chief engineer.[6]

Construction of the Locks

Since the doors of the massive locks had to resist incredible pressure as well as open and close with precision, it was imperative that the lock walls be solidly constructed. They could not shift in the ground. In order to achieve this, the locks were

This picture shows the massive locks under construction at Gatun in February 1910.

designed to be placed directly into the bedrock of the Isthmus and not into the shifting soils above. Survey parties carefully examined the canal route for appropriate sites for the locks. They were located at Gatun on the Atlantic side, and at Pedro Miguel and Sosa on the Pacific side of the Continental Divide. Later, when the ground shifted at Sosa, the lock site was moved to Miraflores.

Although the foundations of the locks were cut into the bedrock, the walls of the locks had to be constructed of rock and cement. Quarries for rock were founded at Porto Bello near Gatun and at Ancon Hill near Panama City. They supplied the needed blocks of stone. They were then moved by barges to the lock construction site. At first, the cement for the masonry work was shipped from the United States, but soon entire cement plants were shipped in pieces to Panama from the United States and set up near the locks. Sand for the concrete was found locally. The concrete work on the locks began at Gatun in August 1909, and at Pedro Miguel and Miraflores on the Pacific side by February 1910.[7]

Each of the lock construction sites was nearly a mile in length. All the dirt and loose rocks were removed from the site to a depth of eighty feet. The workers dug down until they came to a solid rock bottom, and then they leveled that. This was the solid foundation that all the locks were built on. The lock itself was 1,000 feet long and 110 feet wide. Locks were built in pairs, side by side, so that ships could travel each way at the same time. The walls of the locks were constructed of stone and cement blocks. Each wall was taller than a six-story building—eighty-one feet high. The walls themselves contained large chambers, passageways, and monster-sized pipes to pass the water that would fill and empty the lock. To prevent problems in case the bedrock ever cracked, the bottom of the lock was filled with concrete to a depth of ten to fifteen feet. The center wall between each pair of locks was sixty feet wide all the way from top to bottom. The outside walls were forty-five feet wide at the bottom. The final outside wall was constructed as a series of six-foot steps so that at the top, the wall was only eight feet wide.

After they were completed, dirt fill was placed against the outside walls of the locks to make them appear to be cut from the ground around them. They are always at least half full, so the enormity of their size is disguised from the passenger passing through them. At Gatun, three such pairs, three steps, would be constructed. On the Pacific side, there are two pairs at Miraflores and one pair at Pedro Miguel.[8]

The Gatun Locks

The three sets of locks at Gatun contained more material than any other structure in the world. On the floor of the locks, massive steel plates were bolted together to form the shape of the wall to be constructed. The walls were constructed in thirty-six-foot segments. Each segment of the wall took about a week to construct. Sand, gravel, and Portland cement were fed into six giant mixers by a small railroad. The wet concrete was then carried in large buckets to the construction site by another small railroad. Two huge cranes that moved on giant railroad tracks picked up the square buckets that contained twelve thousand pounds of wet concrete and lifted them high into the air above the surrounding jungle. The crane operator sat in a small box on the arm of the crane nearly one hundred feet above the ground. When the buckets were in position above the tall steel forms that stood over eighty feet high above the floor of the locks, they were emptied and returned to the railroad car for another trip.

Nearly thirty-five hundred cubic yards of concrete were poured into the locks during a normal day of construction. As the walls were being built, a network of giant passageways or holes, some eighteen feet in diameter, was constructed within them by using collapsible curved steel forms. These passageways were connected to seventy holes in the floor to allow for the flow of the water that would fill and empty the locks. When a lock was to be filled, a set of valves opened so that water would pour from Gatun Lake above, through these passageways and fill the lock. When the lock was emptied, another set of valves opened and the water flowed down into the sea-level passageway that led back to the sea. It would only take fifteen minutes to fill or half empty a lock.

When the concrete in the walls of the locks was dry, the forms were removed, the cranes were moved thirty-six feet down the line of construction, the steel forms were reassembled, and the pouring of the next segment began. The locks took four years to complete after they started to pour the concrete.[9]

The massive steel gates at each end were the only noticeable moving parts of the locks. Each gate was constructed of two doors, hinged at the outside walls, that met precisely at the center. Each door of the gate was sixty-five feet wide and seven feet thick. The doors were hollow, and when the lock was finished and half filled with water, they would float and thus put less strain on the hinges that held them. Each hinge, weighing more than a ton, was precision made of specially hardened steel that could withstand the strain of several million pounds. As the doors were finished, men would crawl down into them and inspect each rivet that bolted the sections together. When faulty rivets were found, they were cut out and replaced. Each door of the gate was opened and closed by a steel arm connected to a giant wheel-shaped gear, twenty feet in diameter, that was turned by powerful electric motors.

At each end of the lock, two sets of gates were constructed in case one of the sets failed to function or was rammed by a ship. To prevent such a catastrophe, as each ship entered a lock, a steel chain was raised from the floor of the lock by massive electric motors and used to hold the ship away from the gate in front. When the ship was properly positioned in the lock, the chain was lowered back into the lock floor. If the ship went out of control, the chain, more than four hundred feet long, acting as a cushioning bumper, would slowly unwind and stop the ship before it rammed the gate. A ten-thousand-ton ship moving at seven miles an hour could be stopped within seventy feet. It was very unlikely that an accident would occur.

Passing Ships Through the Locks

As they are today, the ships were moved through the locks, not by their own power, but by four locomotives, two pulling the ship from the front, and two others holding it back from the rear. The tracks for these locomotives were built into the top of the lock walls. The locomotives would move the ships at two miles an hour or less. Each locomotive—there were forty for the entire canal—was about thirty feet long and had a cab on each end with duplicate controls and engines so that it could be used in either direction without turning around. In the center of each locomotive, there was a large drum, called a windlass, that carried a coil of eight hundred feet of steel cable that was slowly let out to the ship under its control. The steel cable could be rewound around the windlass, thus pulling the ship along, without the locomotive moving at all.

There was another set of gates approximately halfway along the length of the lock so that ships smaller than six hundred feet long could be passed through the lock, saving the amount of water used. At that time, almost all of the ships in the world were less than six hundred feet long. The savings in water would be substantial if the intermediate gates were used. Almost 26 million gallons of water were needed to raise a ship longer than six hundred feet from sea level to the level of Gatun Lake. That much water was needed again to lower the ship through the locks on the Pacific side of the Continental Divide. All of that water would come from the lake formed by the damming of the Chagres River, and ultimately, from the rainfall each year.[10]

Building the great pyramids in Egypt could not have been a more awe-inspiring sight than the construction of the Panama Canal locks. One worker on the locks remembered:

> Men reported to work early and stayed late, without overtime, . . . I really believe that every American employed would have worked that year without pay, if only to see the first ship pass through the completed Canal. That spirit went down to all the laborers.[11]

The locks on the Pacific side were finished first. The single lock at Pedro Miguel was finished in 1911. The double set of locks at Miraflores was finished in May 1913. The triple set of locks at Gatun on the Atlantic side was successfully tested on September 26, 1913. When Major Goethals was asked the secret of their success, he replied that it was the pride the workers took in their work.[12]

The Gatun Dam

As work on the massive wall of the Gatun Dam progressed, the waters of the lake forming behind the dam rose and covered more of the countryside, soon making low-lying islands of what had been the higher hills in the jungle. By November 1, 1912, Gatun Dam was 90 percent complete and parties of workers were sent into the jungle to move thousands of Indians from their traditional homes, out of the way of the rising waters. Many Indians bitterly resented this forced relocation. "The Americans took awful advantage of the poor people, because they had no one to speak for them," eyewitness Rose van Hardeveld sadly remembered sixty years later. When the waters behind the dam reached the desired level of eighty-five feet, the lake covered over one hundred eighty-five square miles. All of the electricity to power the motors used in the daily operation of the canal was generated by a hydroelectric plant constructed at the spillway of the Gatun Dam.[13]

The Culebra Cut

Work continued at the Culebra Cut from both the Atlantic and Pacific sides and finally, on May 20, 1913,

This photograph depicts the progress being made on the massive Culebra Cut between Gold Hill and Contractor's Hill on December 28, 1912.

near the end of the day's work, the nose of a Pacific Ocean shovel touched the nose of an Atlantic Ocean one. In all, almost 100 million cubic yards of mountain had been removed from the Culebra Cut. The width of the cut at the top was eighteen hundred feet. At the bottom, it measured three hundred feet wide. Over 300 million cubic yards of material had been dug out along the entire route of the finished canal. If all of that material were placed inside a city block, it would rise nearly one hundred thousand feet, or nineteen miles, into the air.[14]

Just as the opening ceremonies for the Canal were being planned, another mountain of mud slid into the

Two steam shovels finally met at the bottom of the Culebra Cut on May 20, 1913.

These are the effects of a mud slide shortly before the opening of the canal on December 3, 1913.

Culebra Cut during the rainy season of 1913. Major Goethals decided to proceed with the flooding of the cut, using the rising waters of Gatun Lake. Once the Culebra Cut was flooded, he would bring floating dredges up the locks and across Gatun Lake to finish the excavation of the cut.

The Canal Finally Opens

A dirt dam, called the Gamboa Dike, had been built at the Atlantic end of the Culebra Cut to hold back the rising waters of Gatun Lake. On October 1, 1913, six large drainpipes from the dike were opened to allow a small flow of water into the Culebra Cut. For ten days dynamite charges were placed in the dike. On October 10, at 2:00 P.M., United States President Woodrow Wilson pushed a button in his office in Washington, D.C. At 2:01 P.M. in Panama, two thousand miles away, the one-hundred-foot center of the Gamboa Dike was blown sky high, scattering mud on the thousands of cheering onlookers. The waters from the lake poured into the cut and in eighteen minutes reached the mud slide. On December 10, 1913, an old French dredge, the *Marmot*, first cleared the way through the slide. An old crane boat, the *Alexander La Valley*, which had been brought up through the Gatun locks to work on the dredging of the Culebra Cut, was passed down to the Pacific side on January 7, 1914. It became the first ship to pass through the Panama Canal.[15]

AFTERWORD

After the official inaugural passage of the U.S.S. *Ancon* through the canal on August 15, 1914, almost all of the canal workers returned to their homes. Hundreds of barracks and supply buildings were dismantled or demolished. William Gorgas left Panama to fight pneumonia among natives employed in the gold mines in South Africa. Major Goethals was named the first governor of the Panama Canal Zone.

The Canal in Operation

The United States Congress set the fee for using the canal at ninety cents for each ton of cargo transported. Things quickly quieted down to a regular routine. The canal was designed to be operated by only 210 employees. There were a few stories covering the opening of the canal in newspapers, but most of the world's attention at the time was focused on World War I, then just beginning. In August 1914, a general conflict among almost all of the nations of Europe began with the assassination of the heir to the Hapsburg empire of Austria-Hungary. It lasted for four years and is known today as World War I.[1]

Work on the canal has never really stopped, especially at the Culebra Cut. When U.S.S. *Ancon* made the inaugural passage, there was only a channel one hundred fifty feet wide that had been dredged from the latest mud slide into the cut. Over the years, the mountains continued to shift and pour mud into the channel. In October 1914, another mud slide entirely blocked the channel in just half an hour. Most of the barge-operated steam shovels that had been used to excavate the sea-level channels of the canal

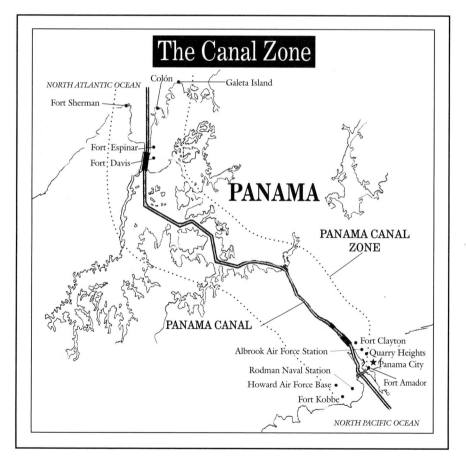

This map shows the Panama Canal and the Canal Zone.

route were moved up to Gatun Lake where they were used continually to excavate the cut and move the mud to remote dumps in Gatun Lake. The next August it happened again. On September 18, 1915, another mud slide closed the canal for seven months. These steam shovels have worked every year at a great expense to keep the cut open. In 1974 one slide dumped nearly a million cubic yards of mud into the cut.[2] In the late 1990s, the price for the annual upkeep of the canal included $450 million for canal operation, which covered periodic overhauls of the lock gates, pumps, locomotives, valves, and other necessary equipment.[3]

Traffic through the canal was light at first. Until the end of World War I in 1918, fewer than two thousand ships passed through the canal each year. By 1925, traffic had doubled to more than four thousand ships a year. By 1940, seven thousand ships a year— nearly twenty each day—passed through the canal. Nightlights were installed after World War II to extend the hours of the canal's operation. By the 1970s, more than fifteen thousand ships used the canal each year. Together they paid a fee of more than $100 million. The average ship pays about ten thousand dollars for its passage. That fee is based on the total tonnage of the ship that passes through the canal. The H.M.S. *Queen Elizabeth II,* an exceptionally heavy ship, which passed through the canal in March 1975, paid a record $42,077.88.

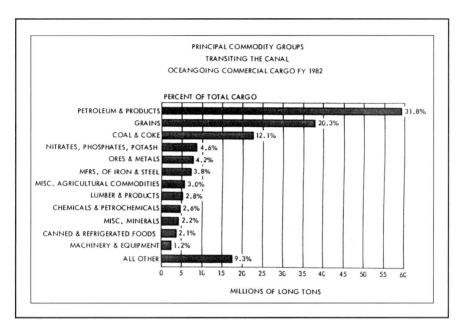

This graph shows the principal kinds of commodities that were transported through the Panama Canal in 1982.

H.M.S. *Queen Mary,* which was launched in 1936, was the first ship constructed that was too large to use the canal. All of the locks of the present canal are 1,000 feet long and 110 feet wide.[4] Obviously, any ship longer or wider than that is too big to use the Panama Canal. These ships must travel around the tip of the continent of South America to complete their journey between the Pacific and Atlantic oceans, just as ships had to do before the canal was built. In recent years, many super tankers that haul enormous quantities of oil to the United States from production sites in Asia have proved too large to pass through the locks of the canal.[5]

Future Expansion of the Canal

In 1996–1997, seventeen thousand cargo ships carrying over 190 million tons of merchandise used the Panama Canal. This was equal to nearly 4 percent of all the shipping traffic in the world. Another 7 percent of the world's shipping would use the canal, but cannot because the ships are too big.

A world conference on expanding the Panama Canal was held in September 1997 at the request of the governments of Panama, Japan, and the United States. Participants made several suggestions for the Panama Canal in the twenty-first century. They suggested that another set of locks be constructed alongside the present ones at a cost of $8.5 billion. These would allow ships of 200,000 tons displacement—three times larger than present limits allow—to use the canal. Another proposal was to construct an entirely new canal, six miles west of the current canal, at a cost of approximately $14.2 billion. This new canal would allow ships of 250,000 tons, four times larger than present limits allow, to pass through Panama.[6]

When the canal was built, it was designed to be protected by military fortifications located at the Atlantic and Pacific ends of the canal. Huge guns with barrels sixteen inches in diameter protected the entrances to the canal. Along the route of the canal, the jungle was allowed to grow right up to the channel, also as a protective measure. At that time, the American Navy was the United States' first line of defense from foreign invasion. The ability to quickly move ships from one coast or ocean to another was important. Today, space satellites and rockets guard the borders of the United States, and the military importance of the canal has diminished.

Conflicts

When the United States participated in Panama's rebellion from Colombia in 1903, it did so in order to gain the rights to build the Panama Canal. The treaty signed between the two countries was written in America and was very advantageous to the United States. The United States claimed that the treaty made the land of the Canal Zone part of United States territory, subject to the laws of the United States, not Panama. Panamanians later declared that the land had only been rented to the United States, not given away. Throughout the history of the canal, the United States has been a large and powerful country, whereas Panama has been a small and poor one. For over seventy years after the treaty, the United States ignored the growing complaints of Panamanians who resented the presence of a foreign army, a foreign language, and a foreign flag to protect the lands of the canal given to the United States by a Frenchman.

In the last one hundred fifty years, the United States has sent its military to Panama many times in order to protect American interests there. For example, in 1856 a dispute between an American and a Panamanian fruit vendor ended in a riot, in which dozens were killed and more than fifty wounded. The

United States government sent the navy to pressure New Granada (now Colombia) into accepting total responsibility for the riot. New Granada bowed before the military pressure and paid compensation for the "Watermelon Incident." Such heavy-handed measures hardly made the United States popular in the eyes of the local population, who were generally proud and patriotic citizens. The United States sent troops to Panama in 1860, 1865, 1868, 1873, twice in 1885, 1900, twice in 1903, 1904, and four times between 1908 and 1920.[7]

On November 3, 1959, during celebrations of Panamanian independence, students in Panama City attacked the American Embassy, destroying an American flag and some local business offices. The rioting mob then marched on the Canal Zone, demanding to raise the Panamanian flag there. They were fired upon by American troops. Forty Panamanians were wounded. In response, President Dwight D. Eisenhower of the United States directed that the Panamanian flag be flown alongside, but below, the United States flag in the Canal Zone.

In 1964, American students at Balboa High School refused to fly the Panamanian flag beside the flag of the United States. Panamanians again rioted in Colón, Panama City, and within the Canal Zone. For several days, United States troops inside the Canal Zone fought against sniper attacks. There were numerous deaths and much destruction on both sides until order was established by the Panama National Guard.

This is Balboa High School, the site of conflicts between Panamanians and American Canal Zone officials.

Diplomatic relations between the two countries were halted. It became obvious that the United States had to renegotiate its presence in Panama.[8]

Returning the Canal Zone to Panama

It took more than fourteen years, but in 1977, under the leadership of United States President Jimmy Carter and General Omar Torrijos Herrera, the military leader of Panama, the two countries created a new agreement about the Panama Canal.

The United States Senate ratified the Panama Canal Treaty in 1978.[9] According to this treaty, the operation and defense of the canal would be shared jointly by the two countries. More than half the land of

PANAMA CANAL TREATY

ARTICLE II

THE REPUBLIC OF PANAMA DECLARES THE NEUTRALITY OF THE CANAL IN ORDER THAT BOTH IN TIME OF PEACE AND IN TIME OF WAR IT SHALL REMAIN SECURE AND OPEN TO PEACEFUL TRANSIT BY THE VESSELS OF ALL NATIONS ON TERMS OF ENTIRE EQUALITY, SO THAT THERE WILL BE NO DISCRIMINATION AGAINST ANY NATION, OR ITS CITIZENS OR SUBJECTS, CONCERNING THE CONDITIONS OR CHARGES OF TRANSIT, OR FOR ANY OTHER REASON, AND SO THAT THE CANAL, AND THEREFORE THE ISTHMUS OF PANAMA, SHALL NOT BE THE TARGET OF REPRISALS IN ANY ARMED CONFLICT BETWEEN OTHER NATIONS OF THE WORLD. . . .[10]

The 1977 Panama Canal Treaty set up the transfer of the canal to Panama in 1999 and guaranteed the permanent neutrality of the canal in times of war.

the Canal Zone would return to Panama. Moreover, the name of the new, smaller zone under the control of the United States was changed. Now it was called the Panama Canal Area. December 31, 1999, was designated as the day when the entire canal, and the area adjoining the canal, would be turned over to Panama for good. Until then, most civil services, including police, fire protection, and schools, were given to Panama to administer. The canal itself was placed under the supervision of a Panama Canal Commission, comprised of members from both Panama and the United States.[11]

War in Panama

In the years after the 1978 treaty, Panama was ruled by a military strong man, General Manuel Noriega, who rose to power after the untimely death of Omar Torrijos Herrera in a mysterious plane crash. Noriega accepted money and arms from the United States and, at the same time, transported illegal shipments of drugs from South America to the United States. He promoted anti-American sentiments among his citizens at the same time that he was on the payroll of the Central Intelligence Agency and the United States Army. The United States government felt the insult and decided to strike back.

Just before 1:00 A.M. on December 20, 1989, Operation Just Cause began to drop a bomb every two minutes for over thirteen hours on targets in Panama City. Billion-dollar, super-secret, F-11A stealth

LAST NIGHT I ORDERED U.S. MILITARY FORCES TO PANAMA. . . . FOR NEARLY TWO YEARS, THE UNITED STATES, NATIONS OF LATIN AMERICA AND THE CARIBBEAN HAVE WORKED TOGETHER TO RESOLVE THE CRISIS IN PANAMA. THE GOALS OF THE UNITED STATES HAVE BEEN TO SAFEGUARD THE LIVES OF AMERICANS, TO DEFEND DEMOCRACY IN PANAMA, TO COMBAT DRUG TRAFFICKING, AND TO PROTECT THE INTEGRITY OF THE PANAMA CANAL TREATY. MANY ATTEMPTS HAVE BEEN MADE TO RESOLVE THIS CRISIS THROUGH DIPLOMACY AND NEGOTIATIONS. ALL WERE REJECTED BY THE DICTATOR OF PANAMA, GEN. MANUEL NORIEGA, AN INDICTED DRUG TRAFFICKER.

LAST FRIDAY, NORIEGA DECLARED HIS MILITARY DICTATORSHIP TO BE IN A STATE OF WAR WITH THE UNITED STATES AND PUBLICLY THREATENED THE LIVES OF AMERICANS IN PANAMA. . . . THAT WAS ENOUGH.[12]

In this speech from December 20, 1989, United States President George Bush explained his reasons for sending America military forces into Panama.